Just Ask Andy

Just Ask Andy

Lori Lee Magoon

ISBN: 1511417099
ISBN 13: 9781511417099

ACKNOWLEDGMENTS

First and foremost, this book is for my dad. I want to thank him for always being there for me. He was my backbone while I went through graduate school. He held my hand while I went through some of the most painful and challenging times in my life. He even believed in me when I did not. Without him, I would not be where I am today.

Ron, it feels as though my life did not begin fully until I met you. Thank you for being the best husband I could ever ask for. I am so deeply and truly in love with you.

Mom, there is never a day that goes by that I do not think of you. I miss you so much but know that you are now at peace and are happy with Nan and Pop.

Brittany, Ryan, and Emily, you are the brightest lights in my life. I am so proud of all of you. I am truly blessed to have such extraordinary children. I love you more than words can say.

Madeline, my beautiful granddaughter, I love you to the moon and back!

My brothers, Dan and Jeff, I love you both!

Andy, my beloved cat! I will always remember you.

My wonderful clients—all of the amazing people who have taught me everything I know about addiction—you all have so much courage, love, and grace. I believe in all of you and pray that you will always see what I see—the beautiful hearts and souls you each possess.

Thank you for trusting me with your thoughts, emotions, and aspirations. It has been a privilege to work with you.

To all who have lost their lives to this devastating disease, I promise you that I will do my best to keep fighting for the rights of those who suffer from addiction.

God bless!

INTRODUCTION

As a master's-level alcohol and drug counselor, licensed mental health clinician, and host of a radio show developed to support individuals in recovery, I have been asked many questions about substance misuse and addiction. Although I have not always been able to give a definitive answer to each inquiry (as life does not often come equipped with definitive answers), I feel confident that I have helped many people who have been impacted either directly or indirectly by substance misuse and addiction.

As a therapist and radio show host, I began to notice that many individuals asked similar questions about substance abuse and addiction. I heard from individuals who struggled with addiction and from friends and family members affected by a loved one's addiction. As I began to recognize these patterns in inquiries, I decided that my clients, as well as others, might benefit from a reference book containing answers to common questions about addiction.

So why use Andy the Cat as my mode of presentation for this book? Like many modern-day marvels, it all began with Facebook. As cat lovers, my husband and I decided that it would be funny to develop a Facebook page for Andy, our lovable cat. After we posted a status update on Andy's Facebook page about his love for catnip, "Andy's addiction" became an ongoing jest. It seemed only natural to use Andy's "addiction" as a means to lighten what we all recognize is a serious and troubling topic.

Substance misuse affects all populations. Even if you are not struggling with substance misuse issues and/or addiction, it is very likely that you have a family member or friend who is. I have been asked hundreds of questions over the years relating to substance misuse, addiction, relapse, and recovery. *Just Ask Andy* is a collection of the most commonly asked questions and answers to those questions from "Andy." I hope this book helps answer any questions you may have and reminds you that if you are affected by substance misuse and addiction, you are not alone, and there is always hope.

The difference between a successful person and others is not a lack of strength, not a lack of knowledge, but rather a lack of will.
—Vince Lombardi

JUST ASK ANDY

Hello, my name is Andy Martel. I guess you could consider me a grateful and sober drug addict. I have gone through a great deal in my life to overcome the struggles of addiction. I am now on the other side and am very happy with who I am today.

My story began five years ago when I went outside for a walk in my mother's herb garden. I came across the most amazing plant named for cats: a plant called catnip. I sniffed, nibbled, scratched, and rolled around on it, experiencing an incredible feeling of euphoria. For the first time in all of my nine lives, I forgot about my problems. I did not think about the day I was taken from my birth mother and my kitten siblings. I did not think about never knowing my real father or about all the other kittens who called me the redheaded stepchild. I did not think about the mouse that had been teasing me, or how my adopted father kicked me off the bed at night and made me sleep on the floor. For the first time in a long time, I felt relaxed and happier than ever.

A couple of weeks went by after the experience in the herb garden, and all I could think about was the feeling I got from that plant. Every day I would find myself thinking about when I would be able to get back outside and enjoy that beautiful plant again.

I knew my adopted mother would not approve of my catnip use, so I had to find a way to get to the garden without her finding out. One day, my mother left to go to her favorite place, Prescott Farms, to get kibble for our dog, Dexter, and I snuck out the door as soon as she opened it to leave. I ran over to the garden as fast as I could and once again enjoyed the euphoric feeling that this plant gave me. I could not get enough of the smell, texture, and taste of catnip.

A couple of days went by, and I couldn't help but notice that a window in the basement was open. I was delighted to find that I could get in and out of the window without my adoptive family knowing. Before I knew it, I was back in the garden on a catnip high—sniffing, nibbling, and rolling. In such moments, nothing else mattered. I had what I wanted and felt the way I had always wanted to feel. I was in love with catnip.

Over time, I began to notice that I needed to sniff, nibble, and roll on the plant a bit more than I did the first time in order to experience the same euphoric effect. It was almost as if I was chasing my first high.

I went out to the garden at every chance I got and was overwhelmed with joy every time I surrounded myself with my favorite herbal plant. From the moment I woke up to the moment my head hit the pillow, all I could think about was catnip. I began to visit the garden daily, and soon I was there two or three times per day. I started to sneak bags full of catnip into the house, and I stashed them behind my litter box.

After a month or two, my adoptive mother's herbal garden became scarce and the catnip plants dwindled. I panicked. I wondered what I would do when the catnip was gone and how I could get more.

I soon found myself scoping out our neighbors' gardens. I had never noticed before, but our neighbors had lots of gardens, including herbal gardens with catnip in them. In my heart, I knew that going into the neighbors' gardens and taking catnip plants was stealing. However, I figured that they wouldn't notice if just a little bit of their catnip was gone.

So, yes, I am ashamed to admit that during the evening hours when no one was looking, I began stealing catnip from our neighbors. I would take a bit from the Hicks, some from the Suttons, a little from the Fords, and a smidge from the O'Neils. Then I found out that the Magoons had three different types of catnip. Score. I was all set. I had all the catnip I could want.

I kept the stolen catnip in plastic bags and hid them behind my litter box. No one knew. No one even questioned it. I had everything under control. I had the world by its tail. I always felt happy; I had a constant sense of euphoria. There was nothing I could not do.

Then things suddenly changed. One day, my adoptive mother announced that the family was going on vacation for a week and that they would leave enough food and water to get me by until they returned. My mother expressed that she did not want me to go outside and told me, "You have been making a habit of disappearing lately, mister. You are to stay in the house because we are leaving soon and want you to be safe." Then she went down to the basement and shut the window that I had been using to get my catnip. *Safe my ass*, I thought to myself. *I am now officially a prisoner in my own home.*

I immediately took stock of my supply and realized that I was running low on nip. I certainly did not have enough to get through more than a day or so, let alone a week! I began to sweat. I wondered what I was going to do. My adoptive mother hugged and kissed me goodbye and said, "You be a good boy! I left you plenty of water and food. We will be back in a week. Love you!"

As I watched my adoptive mother and father walk out the door, I found myself thinking, *Screw you! How the hell am I going to get my fix? Do you understand, woman? I don't have enough stuff to last me!* I ran to the window, pressed my face up against the glass and yelled, "Mom and Dad, please don't leave me! I don't think I'm strong enough to go without my catnip!"

After my parents left, I cried like a kitten for hours. I was in a panic. Finally, I got my head straight and thought about how I was going to handle this dilemma. I counted up the catnip that I had left and decided I would ration it. I knew that I needed to make it last so that I didn't experience withdrawal symptoms.

I quickly asked myself, "Will I get withdrawal symptoms?"

I abruptly realized that I was incapable of rationing my drug of choice when my stash was gone within a day or so. On the first day without catnip, I felt fine. In fact, I did not feel a thing and found myself thinking that my obsession with the magic plant was under control. On the second day without it, I woke up with flu-like symptoms. I began vomiting violently, and the mouse that I had eaten the day before came out in a projectile manner—first the head, then the teeth, then the toes and tail. I later began itching all over, my head and stomach hurt, and I started suffering from diarrhea. I knew my adoptive parents were not going to be happy when they found that I had missed the litter box six times (all within a two-hour period).

I lay on my adoptive parents' bed, where I began throwing up hair balls, cat food, dog food, and a red ribbon. I still have no idea where that red ribbon came from. It felt as though my head were going to explode. I knew if I only had a little bit of catnip (a wee little amount), this feeling would go away. However, I had no access to nip, and the symptoms continued.

There was nothing I could do to relieve how I was feeling. I tried sitting down, lying down, standing up, and walking around. I even tried to drink some water. Nothing helped. I was in this for the long haul, and it was not pretty.

A week went by, and my parents came home. My adoptive mother took one look at me and screamed, "Oh my god, what is wrong with you? We need to bring you to the Raymond Rams Animal Hospital right away!" She ran down the stairs to get the cat carrier, put a towel in it, and gently picked me up and put me in. I did not even have enough energy to fight—an abnormal reaction, as I would generally scream and scratch at the mere sight of the cat carrier.

My mother put me in the car and began driving me to the hospital. I have never been carsick before, but detoxing from catnip and riding in the car did not mix. I began vomiting again, only this time nothing came out. I dry heaved for ten miles.

When we finally got to our destination, my mother took me out of the car and ran frantically into the building. She ran up to the lady at the front desk, and I overheard her say, "I think my cat is dying. Please help him!"

Three nurses in white coats grabbed my carrier and rushed me into a back room. I felt myself being poked and prodded as blood was taken out of my left front paw. I then found myself peeing through a tube and felt something going up my butt.

As I drifted in and out of consciousness, I could hear only a small amount of what the people in the white coats were saying. My veterinarian, Dr. Emanuel George, gave me some medicine that helped me feel relaxed, and I finally was able to get comfortable and fall into a deep sleep.

The next day, I awoke with my adoptive mother by my side. She held my paw and told me that she loved me no matter what. She said the blood tests that the vet took indicated that I was detoxing from catnip. Then she started crying.

"What did I do wrong?" she asked me. "Did I not give you enough love? It was your adoptive father, wasn't it? He never accepted you into the family and favors our dog, Dexter, over you. I warned him about how that could affect you."

Dr. Emanuel George then came into the room and told us about his recommendation that I attend a twenty-eight-day residential program called Follow the Yarn, a program designed for cats addicted to catnip.

All I could think about was how I didn't need to go away and how I could do this on my own. However, my adoptive mother told me that if I didn't go, she would send me to the Franklin Animal Shelter. I overheard my adoptive father say to my mother, "Let's just send him to the shelter! There are plenty of other cats out there without addiction problems. We can find a cute little kitten, one much cuter than this drug addict."

After overhearing my parents' conversation, I decided to say yes to the catnip program. I knew that if they gave me away, I would end up as one of those pound cats who sit in a cage crying to visitors to please take them home. I knew that with the tartar forming on my teeth, my big belly, and the white hair around my face, I was no longer an adorable kitten.

The catnip program was not as bad as I thought. I was surprised how many different cats I met. Male, female, young, old, tigers, lions, Maine coons, Bengals, and domestic house cats. I even met a couple of Persians named Brittany and Emily—who I might add were a bit on the snotty side—and a cougar named Karli. Even though Karli was a little older than me, I found her delicious. I also met a real cool cat named Ryan. He was gracious enough to share his ball of string with me. We must have batted that thing around for hours every night before bed.

I did learn one thing for sure: this catnip addiction does not discriminate, and any cat can end up addicted by crossing the fe-line into addiction. Follow the Yarn taught me all about substance use, abuse, and addiction. I became well versed in triggers and relapse prevention, and I learned that many cats overdose when they relapse because they tend to go right back to using the same amount they were using when they stopped, and their bodies do not have a chance to build up a tolerance.

At Follow the Yarn, I also learned about mental illness. I realized that I suffer from depression and post-traumatic stress disorder stemming from when I was taken from my birth mother. I also learned that I suffer from an attachment disorder because I was taken from my mother at an early age and did not learn to attach properly.

Of all the things I learned at Follow the Yarn, the most important was that I am not a bad cat. I have a good heart, and the disease of addiction took me when I was not looking. I developed a treatment plan, a relapse-prevention plan, and a safety plan. I attended Catnip Anonymous (CNA) groups and learned how their twelve-step program worked. I even found a sponsor whom I still have to this day! By the time I was discharged from Follow the Yarn's twenty-eight-day addiction residential program, I was a new cat. Thank god that I had eight lives left to live drug-free.

After being discharged, I went home with my family, and we all began attending family therapy. Together, we learned that addiction is a family disease. My mother learned about codependence and enabling, and my father and I talked about the issues we had with each other. For the first time since I had been adopted, my father hugged me and told me that he loved me. The dog...well, the dog, that's another story, and I would rather not get into it at this time.

Along with family counseling at Self-empowerment-NH, I also began attending individual counseling at Bernier Counseling and worked on my mental health issues. I continued with CNA and spoke to my sponsor weekly, and sometimes even daily. In fact, I became so confident within the sponsoring process that I began sponsoring five individuals myself. I was also glad that my parents went to a weekly support group called We Are without Shame. This group is for family members of people with addiction issues.

I can honestly say that my life has changed for the better. I am a happy cat now, one who enjoys life to the fullest. I won't lie—I do sometimes look out at the herb garden and fantasize about jumping in for old time's sake. However, I quickly catch myself and try to remember where catnip brought me—down a dark path that almost took my life and my family away from me.

The story of Andy's addiction was developed sequentially to help explain what it feels like for someone who suffers from addiction. No matter what the drug of choice—catnip, cocaine, heroin, cannabis, or any other mind-altering substance—most people are likely to go through a similar series of events. Andy is among the SMALL amount of folks who are successful the first time around in treatment. Most people go back and forth from relapse to sobriety for months or even years, and some lose the battle with the deadly disease called addiction.

You are only what you think and that is all.
—Lori Magoon

Andy's story:

(1) Introduced to his drug of choice
Andy tried his drug of choice and liked it right away. He even said to himself, "This is the feeling I have always been looking for."

(2) Began using it more and more
Andy started using it once a week, then twice a week, then eventually every day. The amount he used changed too. At first, one hit got him high; over time he began to realize that he needed more and more to get the same effect.

(3) Began to think about his drug of choice constantly and dreamed of his next fix
Andy started noticing that the number one thing in his life was catnip. It was the first thing he thought about when he woke up in the morning and the last thing he thought about when he went to bed. Even while he was in the process of using catnip, he began to obsess about the next time he would be able to use it. He worried that he did not have enough to get him through the day.

(4) Began to lie, cheat, and steal to get his drug
Andy started lying to his mother about his whereabouts. He knew that she would not approve of what he was doing, so he started to get sneaky. He also began stealing from the neighbors. He figured that he would not get caught and did not think about the consequences.

(5) Realized he was hooked and was scared of the notion of detox
Andy accepted the fact that he was addicted to catnip when he couldn't get what he needed and didn't feel "normal" without it.

(6) Went through detoxification process
Andy was unable to get catnip, and because of this, his body began to detox from the substance. He was very ill and suffered severe, flu-like symptoms.

(7) Family found out about his problem and wanted him to get help
Andy's family learned of his addiction and told him to get treatment.

(8) Denial of needing help
Andy was in denial of his problem and refused to get help. He kept on telling himself he didn't really have a problem and could take care of himself. He believed that if he wanted to stop, he would stop.

(9) Family told him to get into rehab or he was out of the family
Andy's family insisted that he be admitted into a twenty-eight-day substance abuse treatment program, or they would make him move out of their home.

(10) Went to treatment apprehensively
Andy agreed to go because he was afraid he would have to go to the shelter if he was not admitted to a twenty-eight-day substance abuse treatment program.

(11) Ended up liking rehab
Within a week or so, Andy started to settle into the treatment program and became comfortable.

(12) Accepted sobriety
Andy began wanting to be sober and started taking his treatment seriously. He started listening to his counselor, and he joined in on psycho-educational groups. He developed a relapse-prevention plan.

(13) Released from rehab
Andy completed the twenty-eight-day substance abuse residential program and moved back home.

(14) Continued with a twelve-step program and obtained a sponsor
Andy continued with a twelve-step program and began attending the program regularly. He also found a sponsor.

(15) Family went to family counseling
Andy and his family went to family counseling to learn how to communicate about Andy's addiction. They learned about the signs and symptoms of early relapse and what Andy's triggers were. They discussed how Andy's addiction affected the family. This helped the family heal.

(16) Attended individual substance abuse counseling
Andy went to a substance abuse counselor on his own to work on relapse-prevention skills and to work through some mental health issues.

(17) Andy stayed sober and became a twelve-step sponsor
Andy now lives a happy and productive life. He is proud of his accomplishment of staying sober, and he supports others in recovery.

INSPIRATIONAL THOUGHTS

No one is going to hand me success. I must go out and get it myself. That's why I'm here. To dominate. To conquer. Both the world and myself.
—Unknown

People who succeed have momentum. The more they succeed, the more they want to succeed, and the more they find a way to succeed. Similarly, when someone is failing, the tendency is to get on a downward spiral that can even become a self-fulfilling prophecy.
—Tony Robbins

Every great dream begins with a dreamer. Always remember, you have within you the strength, the patience, and the passion to reach for the stars to change the world.
—Harriet Tubman

Here are some common questions that have been asked to me in the past:

QUESTION:

Hi Andy,
I went to counseling and did not feel comfortable talking to my counselor. We just did not seem to hit it off. Is this normal, or is there something wrong with me?
Dislike

ANSWER:

Dear Dislike,

Not every counselor is going to work with every client. You have the right to try out different ones. If one does not work for you, do not waste your time with that counselor. Move on to the next. Keep on doing this until you find the right one. Many clinicians will do an interview process over the phone, and some will even offer the first appointment for free. Good for you for looking for help.

Two roads diverged in a wood, and I—I took the one less traveled by.
And that has made all the difference.
—Robert Frost

QUESTION:

Dear Andy,

My twenty-eight-year-old son has gone to a substance abuse residential program four times in the past three years because of his addiction to methamphetamines. Each time I hope that he will finally get better, but each time I am let down. I am not sure if I should expect him to ever get sober. What are your thoughts?

Devastated.

ANSWER:

Dear Devastated,
I am so sorry to hear that this is happening to both you and him. First, I will say that it can take several tries for a person to get sober. I like to think of it this way: each time a person goes to treatment, we are planting seeds that will grow when that person is ready. We are not in control of what that person does, but we can believe in him or her and in his or her recovery. I do hate to admit that for some people, this can be an ongoing struggle that can span a lifetime. They may need to continuously work on recovery. They may go through a series of relapses, denial of relapses, acceptance, and a desire to get help—followed by getting help, attaining sobriety for a while, and then relapsing again. This does not mean that they are weaker or do not want sobriety. It is just that this is a disease that tends to hijack our brains. It is devastating to watch. I hate seeing an addicted person's loved ones going through this because it hurts the whole family unit. It is important for you to understand the process and accept that this may go on for a long time. Sorry. Please stay strong.

Whatever the mind of man can conceive and believe, it can achieve.
—Napoleon Hill

QUESTION:

Dear Andy,

I recently got out of a twenty-eight-day substance abuse residential program and am now trying to go back to living a normal life. Everything seems weird to me. Sobriety was easy while I was in rehab. Now everywhere I turn, I am reminded of using heroin. What should I do?

Sincerely,
Junk Box

ANSWER:

Hello,
First, I am not going to call you Junk Box. I believe that it is impera-tive for you not to call yourself a junky. You are a human being with a disease. It is normal to feel odd when you first get out of rehab. You've spent twenty-eight days living in a society where there is support 24-7, each person in the facility is working toward sobriety, and triggers are at a low. Then you go out into the world, and there are triggers everywhere you look. Some people are triggered by emotions, some people by places, and some by things. The key is learning to deal with your triggers. If I were you, I would consider going to a substance abuse intensive outpatient program (IOP). Most IOPs meet three to four times a day for three to four hours each time. They usually offer individual counseling too. This is a perfect step down from a residential program. This will help you get back into your daily life gradually and help give you the support where it may be needed.
I wish you the best!

The most common way people give up their power is by thinking they don't have any.
—Alice Walker

QUESTION:

Dear Andy,

I am five years clean from opioids and recently learned that I have to have knee surgery. I am worried that I will end up relapsing if I need to take pain medication after my surgery. What should I do?

In Pain

ANSWER:

Dear In Pain,

This is a common problem. Of course we recommend you not take your drug of choice once sober to prevent relapse, but sometimes you do not have a choice. You may benefit from talking to your surgeon or your medical doctor to come up with a relapse-prevention plan. If you are prescribed painkillers, you can have a loved one dispense them to you. You could also benefit from talking with your doctor about being on this substance for as little time as possible. I have had people meet with me for counseling while they went through this process to help prevent relapse. They may see me while they are prescribed the opioids and then for a short time afterward to make sure that their thought process is accurate. This disease likes to hijack the brain, so we need to stay on top of the way we think and not allow the addiction to trick us into relapse. Most people who have had substance misuse problems describe having two personalities—the using self and the clean self. They explain that there is a constant fight between the two, and it is IMPERATIVE not to allow the using self to take over. This is done by something called cognitive behavioral therapy. This teaches us to listen to our thoughts and challenge negative ones. Good for you for being proactive and keeping yourself safe!

Every strike brings me closer to the next home run.
—Babe Ruth

QUESTION:

Dear Andy,
I feel so terrible about myself. I know that I have let everyone down because I have relapsed time after time. Every time I say I am going to stay clean, I mean what I say, and then I no longer like being sober and then relapse. UGH!
Sad Girl

ANSWER:

Dear Sad Girl,

You are definitely in a tough place, but I will say that many people go through a similar process. Most people do want sobriety in the beginning. They may get sober, love being sober, and go through something we call the "honeymoon stage." This is when sobriety is new and everything seems wonderful! Then sometimes what can happen is reality hits and sobriety gets harder. The newly sober person begins to feel emotions and might start to feel irritated and depressed. This is a time when a person may relapse. This is why it is imperative to gain treatment for both the addict and his or her family while he or she is in early recovery. I suggest to most families to learn what the addicted person's triggers are and the early signs of relapse. Statistics show that most people relapse emotionally two to three weeks before they relapse physically. If the whole family learns the signs and symptoms of early relapse, it may be prevented. You deserve to have a happy life. Please do not give up.

You can never cross the ocean until you have the courage to lose sight of the shore.
—Christopher Columbus

QUESTION:

Dear Andy,
My adult son just got out of a twenty-eight-day residential program. This will be his fifth time in the past two years. Each time, I promise myself that I will not let him come home, and each time I give in because the thought of him living out on the streets just kills me. He gets out in three weeks and is hoping to come home. I am truly at a loss for what to do.
Please Help

ANSWER:

Dear Please Help,

I once heard at a twelve-step program I attended that the definition of insanity is doing the same thing over and over again and expecting a different result. What this tells me is that you may benefit from finding an alternative route. Have you thought about a sober house or halfway house? This is a house that is designed for people who recently came out of a substance abuse residential program and do not feel ready to go out into the world. Many houses have counselors and may offer a substance abuse intensive outpatient program. Some may even help residents find employment. I would suggest looking in your area to see what is available. I also would talk to the residential program that your son is currently in and see if they can recommend something that may help him. Most programs will help line up housing and/or treatment for clients before they leave the program.

God bless you and your son.

Whatever you can do, or dream you can, begin it. Boldness has genius, power, and magic in it.

—Johann Wolfgang von Goethe

QUESTION:

Dear Andy,

In your story, you said that you began using catnip to feel normal, not to get high. Can you please tell me what went through your mind as you continued to use your drug of choice despite knowing that you were not enjoying the high anymore and only using so you would not get sick?

Anonymous

ANSWER:

Dear Anonymous,
It took me some time before I realized that I was using in order to maintain normalcy, rather than to achieve the high itself. I know that may sound odd, but when the catnip took over my mind, using it regularly was all I could think about. I did not even notice that I had crossed the line into addiction until I was made to face my demons and the hell of detox. In the back of my mind, I knew that if I stopped using daily, I might detox. However, I did not know that for sure until I went a couple of full days catnip-free. It was then that I realized catnip's role in helping me remain "normal" and not get sick.

Your life is a garden. Your thoughts are the seeds. If your life isn't awesome, you're watering the weeds.
—Unknown

QUESTION:

Dear Andy,

I am addicted to heroin and cannot stop. The first thing I think about when I wake up and the last thing I think about before bed is heroin. The only thing I care about is heroin. I have cheated, stolen, and have even sold my body to use heroin. I don't know what to do. Please help.

Sincerely,

Lost

ANSWER:

Hello, Lost,

The first thing I want to tell you is that you can't do this on your own. I recommend that you turn to your family and/or friends and ask them for help. Also, it could be very beneficial to contact your medical doctor and explain your symptoms because your doctor may be able to assist you in seeking a detoxification program. You should also ask your doctor to recommend a substance abuse professional. A substance abuse professional can conduct an assessment to provide recommendations on the level of care that would suit you best. Levels of care include substance misuse detoxification programs, substance misuse outpatient counseling, substance misuse intensive outpatient programs, and twenty-eight-day residential substance misuse programs. You may even be a candidate to begin a suboxone maintenance program or to use a medication called naltrexone to alleviate cravings, which can help to prevent relapse. Hang tight, my friend. What you are going through is very difficult. However, you have already taken the first step—you have realized that you have a problem. Don't do this alone! Get the support you need and deserve.

Don't carry your mistakes around with you. Instead place them under your feet and use them as stepping-stones.
—Unknown

QUESTION:

Dear Andy,
My brother has been showing signs of using mind-altering substances. He has been sneaking out of the house and staying out all night. He has been very aloof. He is just not himself. How can I ask him if he has a substance abuse problem without him being angry with me?
Sincerely,
Not Sure

ANSWER:

Dear Not Sure,

I guess there is no way to guarantee that he will not be angry with you. If you suspect that he may be using mind-altering substances, why not ask? He may not be honest with you, but it may help matters if you bring it out in the open. I recommend becoming educated on the subject. You may benefit from learning about codependency and enabling. These terms are used to help explain how loved ones can sometimes support the addicted person's substance misuse in order to feed their own needs. One reason loved ones may do this is because they may be afraid the addicted person will leave if they confront that person. Most important, please consider how angry you think your brother may get if you question him. If you feel that you are not safe and are putting yourself in danger by asking, you may want to seek support from family members, friends, and substance misuse and/or mental health professionals.

Serenity comes from trading expectations for acceptance.
—Anonymous

QUESTION:

Dear Andy,
I have been clean from cocaine for two months, and I am miserable. I miss using cocaine and feel depressed. I know cocaine is different from catnip, but I am hoping you can relate. Did you feel the same when you were in early recovery?
Sincerely,
Miserable

ANSWER:

Dear Miserable,
I can absolutely relate to your situation. I've experienced many ups and downs in early recovery. I must say that addiction is addiction is addiction. It is normal to have symptoms of depression, to feel tired or lethargic, and to have symptoms of anxiety, such as irritability, mood swings, and trouble sleeping. In early recovery, a person's brain chemistry is completely out of whack. The chemicals are working to become normalized and to recalculate your happy brain chemicals, such as dopamine, serotonin, and others. I would suggest visiting your doctor and talking about how you feel. The doctor may suggest an antidepressant for you. Also, attending individual substance misuse counseling and attending a twelve-step program with a sponsor may help you through this time. If you do not like twelve-step programs, you may want to try a SMART Recovery group. They are education-based and do not require sponsorship. I will say that I have seen people have much success working in group sessions with other people who suffer from the same problem. One can never seek enough support in early recovery. I wish you the best of luck and prosperity!

The only difference between a good day and a bad day is your attitude.

QUESTION:

Dear Andy,

I have been clean for four months and am very proud of my accomplishments. I am ashamed to say that I lied to my family when I was using mind-altering substances and stole from them from time to time. I am clean now and doing great. My question for you is this: When will my family trust me again? Every time I leave the house, they ask me where I am going and seem suspicious when I give them my answer. They still will not allow me to carry money because they are afraid I will use it to buy drugs. I even caught them looking through my cell phone. What can I do?

Sincerely,

Anonymous

ANSWER:

Hello, Anonymous,

First, congratulations for being clean. Good for you! I am sorry to hear that you are going through this with your family because it must be very discouraging. I have heard similar complaints from many people in early recovery. However, in your family's defense, you have lied to them on numerous occasions and have even stolen from them. It will take your family time to forgive and trust you again. You need to be patient and willing to consider your family's point of view. You may benefit from talking to them about how you are feeling and also be willing to listen to what they have to say. I highly recommend family counseling as a means to communicate your concerns and feelings. It is imperative for you to try to understand where they are coming from—not to cause you guilt and shame but for you to take responsibility for your past actions. This will help you heal as a person and can help all of you heal as a family unit. I hope you experience a great deal of happiness from this day forward. Remember that patience is the key!

QUESTION:

Hi Andy,
Over the past two months, three different people have told me that I have a "problem" with alcohol. I do not agree with them. How would I know that I do have a "problem"?
Sincerely,
No Problems Here

ANSWER:

Hello, No Problems Here,

Many times other people can see things that we cannot. Why do they say you have a problem? What symptoms are they pointing out? It might be beneficial for you to search the keywords *substance misuse*, *abuse*, and *addiction* on the Internet. Recognizing the differences between these terms may help answer your question. It is normal for a person who has a problem to be in denial. How often do you drink? How much do you drink? Do you drink in spurts? Do you drink even though there are consequences? Do you have a personality change when you drink? Do you avoid social events because you would rather be in a place where you are OK to drink? Do you set out to drink only a few drinks and end up drinking more than planned? Do you have blackouts when you drink? Do you have hangovers? Do you notice that you need more and more alcohol to get the same effect? Do you get shaky when you do not drink? My questions could go on and on. There are different kinds of alcoholics. We tend to visualize a person walking down the street dressed in baggy, dirty clothes and swigging from a paper bag. Not every alcoholic looks like that. Some alcoholics go to work every day and only drink in the evenings, some do not drink all week and binge on the weekends, some hide their drinking and drink primarily alone, and some go weeks and maybe even months without drinking and then go on a bender. It is all about the substance taking control over your mind, body, and spirit. Once that happens, you may cross the line into dependency. No one wants to believe or admit that he or she may not have control over substances. You may benefit from contacting a substance abuse professional and asking for guidance.

Remember, working with a counselor is confidential, and whatever you say during your sessions will not leave that office. I hope this helps. I wish you happiness, my friend, and I hope you find what you are looking for.

You never really understand a person until you consider things from his point of view.
—Harper Lee

QUESTION:

Hello, Andy,
I am twenty-four years old and began drinking when I was sixteen years old with my two best friends. Why am I an alcoholic and they are not?
Sincerely,
Confused

ANSWER:

Dear Confused,

I wish I could answer that question. Some people can drink on occasion and never develop a problem while other people drink and become alcoholics. There are so many theories about addiction. Many people say a person is more apt to become an alcoholic or drug addict if there is a family history of addiction. They also say that if substances are readily available in a person's environment, he or she is more likely to become addicted. Another theory is that if a person has a mental illness such as anxiety, depression, bipolar disorder, or attention-deficit disorder, he or she is at higher risk to become dependent on mind-altering substances as a form of self-medicating. They also say the younger a person begins to use mind-altering substances, the more likely it is that he or she may become dependent. The good news is that since you believe and accept that you have a problem, you can begin the journey of recovery. Best wishes to you!

Everyone tells you what's good for you. They don't want you to find your own answers. They want you to believe theirs.
—Dan Millman

QUESTION:

Dear Andy,
I was recently charged with a DWI (Driving While Intoxicated) and was instructed to attend aftercare. I have no idea what this means. Can you please help?
Sincerely,
Desperate

ANSWER:

Hello, Desperate,
Yikes. A DWI is a tough thing to go through. Depending on your state, aftercare could mean a number of things. In New Hampshire, where I live, aftercare may mean substance misuse residential treatment, a substance misuse intensive outpatient program, or substance misuse outpatient counseling. New Hampshire requires you to contact an impaired driver substance misuse professional (IDSP). The IDSP will evaluate you by giving you a variety of tests. He or she may ask you to attend a twenty-hour DWI education program or suggest that you go to counseling with an IDSP-approved licensed alcohol and drug counselor. If you are unsure, I would recommend calling your state bureau of alcohol and drug services and asking them to provide you with the proper information. I have heard of people automatically going into substance abuse counseling because they thought that was what the state required them to do, and then they found out that they were supposed to do something different. This cost them time and money and created aggravation. I suggest you find out exactly what your state requires for aftercare and complete it in a timely manner. Best of luck to you.

We fail to realize that mastery is not about perfection. It's about a process, a journey. The master is the one who stays on the path day after day, year after year. The master is the one who is willing to try, and fail, and try again, for as long as he or she lives.
—George Leonard

QUESTION:

Dear Andy,

I am thirty-one years old and have finally accepted the fact that my mother is an alcoholic. I told her how I felt, and she refused to admit that she has a problem. Can you please tell me what I can do to help her?

Sincerely,

Scared

ANSWER:

Dear Scared,

You should be proud of yourself for being supportive toward your mother. The best thing you can do for her is to get help yourself. It is important for you to learn about addiction, codependency, and enabling. You can join an Al-Anon twelve-step program, go to a SMART Recovery family group, or attend mental health or substance abuse counseling. One important thing I have learned while working with loved ones of people with addiction is this: "You can lead a horse to water, but you cannot make him drink." That is to say, we cannot make a person do something that the person does not want to do. I have had much success when I meet people where they are in their addiction. It's key to tell your mother that you think she "may" have a problem. It's important to tell her that you are not judging her and are trying to understand what she is going through. You may want to express that you love her dearly, and you can imagine she is in pain and may be drinking to self-medicate. I would suggest learning a technique called motivational interviewing. There are many books on this subject. This technique helps people with addiction feel understood and more comfortable talking about how they are feeling. It also gives them permission to come to these conclusions on their own. When we tell a person that he or she has a problem and needs to stop using his or her drug of choice or else, it can make that person defensive and may close the lines of communication completely. Please don't judge your mother. Love her unconditionally. No one wakes up one day and says, "I want to be an alcoholic." It happens gradually. The addiction can be very painful for her and for other people who are involved. Please get the help and support you need to get through this. This is a family disease, and it can take many hostages. Sending you positive thoughts and energy.

Life has three rules: Paradox, Humor, and Change.

- *Paradox: Life is a mystery; don't waste your time trying to figure it out.*
- *Humor: Keep a sense of humor, especially about yourself. It is a strength beyond all measure*
- *Change: Know that nothing ever stays the same.*

—Dan Millman

QUESTION:

Dear Andy,

I am a college student and am addicted to cough syrup. It started when I began taking NyQuil, and now I have been using DSM from the grocery store. I can't stop. Please tell me what I can do to get help.
Sincerely,
Frantic

ANSWER:

Dear Frantic,
You should be afraid. Dextromethorphan (DSM) can be deadly. I would recommend contacting your medical doctor immediately and talking to family members and reaching out to any other support system you may have. You may also benefit from contacting a substance misuse professional for additional support. I know this is very difficult for you, and you cannot do this alone. I am so happy to hear that you are willing to look at this problem and are expressing an interest in stopping. When you stop using the syrup, you may feel lethargic or have insomnia, or you may experience depression, anxiety, and mood swings. Many young people use DSM because it is sold in stores without a prescription. We have seen an increase in the number of young people addicted to this substance over the past five or ten years. There have been many deaths from people misusing DSM. My wish is to get the word out to parents, children, and the public about the dangers of this substance. I am with you in spirit.

You are only what you think you are.
—Anonymous

QUESTION:

Dear Andy,
My twenty-year-old son is addicted to heroin. He said he has not used in two months. I found a needle and a baggy filled with brown powder in his room. What should I do? Why can't he just stop? Is this my fault? Did I do something wrong as a parent?
Sincerely,
Freaked Out

ANSWER:

Dear Freaked Out,

This must be very scary for you. I would first suggest contacting a substance misuse professional to learn about substance misuse and addiction. Joining Al-Anon or a SMART Recovery family group or other support network such as the Families without Shame can help educate and support you. Education is the key component for your son's recovery. So many parents are going through the same thing right now! What would happen if you confronted your son? He might lie and deny that he has a problem, or he may express thanks for allowing him to release his secret. No matter what, having the "elephant in the room" by making believe there is not a problem is an unhealthy environment for both you and your son. Heroin is one of the most difficult substances to quit because of the strength of physical dependency. Detoxing from this substance can be extremely painful. He may experience vomiting, diarrhea, sweats, fever, and chills. He may have pain in his joints and feel as though he has flu-like symptoms times one hundred. I have had many heroin addicts tell me they would "rather die than feel the effects of detoxing from heroin again." Your son may need to be hospitalized while going through this process so he does not become dehydrated. If you can understand how he is genuinely feeling, you may understand his addiction more accurately. This does not give him permission to continue his use, but it does help you to understand what he is going through and the hold his addiction has over him. I have had many parents take this personally and even blame themselves for their child's addiction. I have sat with lots of parents and witnessed tears of sadness, guilt, shame, and remorse. Many parents feel that the addiction came from something they did or did not do. Please try to look at this more objectively and understand that there are many children addicted to heroin or other mind-altering substances. There is an epidemic in our country. We need to stand together and talk to our legislators about the effects of addiction and the need for funding to create more substance misuse prevention and treatment in the United States. Wishing you positive energy.

Authentic abundance comes when you have balanced everything in your life as best as you can. That includes giving away what you have too much of.
—Derek O'Neill

QUESTION:

Dear Andy,
I am a twenty-one-year-old college student. My mother died of cancer two years ago. Soon after my mother's death, my father began drinking alcohol and is now drinking daily. I don't know what to say to him to get him to stop. Please tell me what to do!
Sincerely,
Help Me

ANSWER:

Dear Help Me,
I am sorry to hear that you are going through so much for someone so young. I hope you have support from family members or counselors at school. There are support groups you could get involved in, such as Al-Anon or SMART Recovery family groups. I always recommend meeting people where they are in their addiction. Why is your father drinking? What does he get out of drinking? Is he self-medicating? Does drinking help him escape from the pain of losing his wife? The answers to these questions may help him become sober. I wish there was a way to put a mirror up to him while you ask him the above questions so he could come to the conclusion for himself. If you tell him to stop without asking him what the substance is doing for him, he may become defensive and not want to communicate with you or anyone else. Old school substance abuse counseling used to recommend "tough love," telling a person that he or she needs to stop or you won't be in his or her life anymore. There still may be some cases where this is necessary, but more and more we are learning that if we understand *why* a person uses, and we discuss this with the person in a nonjudgmental way, the person is more apt to be open to discussion. You are taking on a great deal. You have lost your mother and appear to now be afraid of losing your dad too. Please do not take this task on alone. Please ask for help and possibly get some counseling for yourself. You have been through more than a person at your age should go through. This is the time when you should be enjoying your life and planning for your future, not taking responsibility for others. Thinking of you and wishing you the best.

Give up defining yourself—to yourself or to others. You won't die. You will come to life. And don't be concerned with how others define you. When they define you, they are limiting themselves, so it's their problem. Whenever you interact with people, don't be there primarily as a function or a role, but as the field of conscious presence. You can only lose something that you have, but you cannot lose something that you are.
—Eckhart Tolle

QUESTION:

Dear Andy,

I am an alcoholic and drink every night. I have considered attending Alcoholics Anonymous (AA), but I have a social phobia and have trouble going to places where there are a lot of people I don't know. I am suffering deeply. Is there something you can suggest to help me?
Sincerely,
Shy

ANSWER:

Dear Shy,
I feel your pain. I too was shy at one point in my life and understand how overwhelming large groups can be. When getting sober, it is imperative to contact your medical doctor, as detoxing can sometimes be dangerous. Once you have spoken to your doctor, you may benefit from individual substance abuse counseling. This may be a good start for you, and with time, you may gain the confidence you need to be comfortable in a group setting (if this is what you choose to do). While in counseling, you may find value in learning how you became an alcoholic, what it means to be an alcoholic, what intoxication does for you, and what your triggers are that cause you to drink. You may want to create a relapse-prevention plan and a recovery plan. Most important, you will learn that you are not a bad person because you are an alcoholic; you are human, and anyone can become an alcoholic by crossing the line of addiction. Good for you for taking the first step of recovery and reaching out for help. No one can do this alone. You deserve to have a happy and healthy life.

Take chances; make mistakes. That's how you grow. Pain nourishes your courage. You have to fail in order to practice being brave.
—Mary Tyler Moore

QUESTION:

Dear Andy,
I caught my sixteen-year-old son with a bag of marijuana. What can I do to get him to stop?
Sincerely,
Against Marijuana

ANSWER:

Dear Against Marijuana,

As a parent, it can be terrifying to find that your child is using mind-altering substances. The first thing I would do is bring the issue out in the open and tell your son that you found the marijuana. Your son may say that the drugs are not his (most kids will say this), he may get angry, or he may be completely open and tell you that he likes smoking pot and that the substance is not hurting him. Be ready for a selection of comments. Many young adults believe that marijuana is not addictive, will not hurt them, and is completely safe. I always hear this one: "It is safer than alcohol and should be legal." First and foremost, marijuana is not legal in most states, and if someone gets caught with this substance, that person can get arrested and end up with a criminal record. Marijuana can cause a person to become unmotivated and can damage brain chemistry; statistics have shown that adolescents who use cannabis regularly are likely to lose seven to eight IQ points. That's a lot! This substance is DEFINITELY addictive. You may benefit from becoming educated about cannabis abuse and addiction. You can find an abundance of information on the Internet. You are not alone. Many parents share your concerns. Thinking of you!

I'll give you a simple reason why you need to relax and go with the flow. It just ain't worth getting bothered over something you don't have any control over.
—Hayley Hobson

QUESTION:

Hello, Andy,
My elderly father is an alcoholic. I am mostly concerned because he takes medication and mixes his medication and alcohol. I am afraid to say anything to him because I am fearful he will get mad at me. Do you have any recommendations?
Sincerely,
Adult Child

ANSWER:

Hello, Adult Child,
I am sorry to hear about your issue with your father. You may benefit from becoming educated on the dangers of mixing medication and alcohol. Mixing the two can be deadly. You could try contacting your father's medical doctor. Keep in mind that if his doctor does not have a signed release of information on file, he cannot disclose information per HIPAA laws. However, that does not stop him from listening to what you have to say. When you say your father may become angry, do you mean he may become violent? If so, I recommend that you seek support from other family members, friends, or mental health/substance abuse professionals and his medical doctor. You should not do this alone. I hope this helps. Take care.

Angels fly because they take themselves lightly; devils fall because of their gravity.
—G. K. Chesterton

QUESTION:

Dear Andy,
My wife is an alcoholic and is in denial. She drinks daily and at times has blackouts. Her worst episode yet was when she got angry with me because I did not want her to drive. She snuck away with her car keys and did not come back until the next day. When she did return, the truck she had been driving had a large dent in the side of it, and she said she did not know where the dent came from. Every time I talk to her, she will not discuss her drinking problem. I am considering leaving her but want to look at all options before doing so. Can you please give me some guidance?
Sincerely,
Mr. Denial

ANSWER:

Dear Mr. Denial,

You are certainly in a tough position. What supports do you have available? Do you have family members and friends that you can talk to? Do you have people to support you as you go through this process? As I have said many times before, this is a disease that affects whole families. You may want to get in touch with a substance misuse or mental health clinician to get some information on codependency and enabling. You also may want to join Al-Anon and/or a SMART Recovery family group. You may even benefit from marriage counseling with a clinician who has experience working in the addiction field. Unfortunately, it may take a significant event for your wife to finally break through her denial. Many times it takes a DWI, divorce, loss of child custody, health concerns, or loss of a job for an alcoholic to come to terms with his or her dependency problem. Natural consequences have a way of waking us up, and this may be what your wife is waiting for. Please remember that you can't do this on your own. Take care, and thanks for sharing!

When you analyze the family belief system, you can begin to see that much of what you experience as "the way it is" is just the way it was in your family of origin and that you can choose a different way of seeing yourself and your potential. Once you understand how it was, you can decide how you want it to be.
—Terri Cole

QUESTION:

Dear Andy,

I am addicted to cigarettes and was diagnosed with emphysema. I was told that I needed to quit smoking because if I don't, my emphysema will get worse. I have tried everything, including Chantix, nicotine gum, and nicotine patches. However, when I stop smoking, I get an overwhelming feeling of anxiety and stress. Can you give me any other avenues to help me quit smoking?

Best,

Don't Want to Be Sick

ANSWER:

Dear Don't Want to Be Sick,

There are many avenues for quitting smoking. First and foremost, you may benefit from contacting your medical doctor or psychiatrist to see if they can help you with withdrawal symptoms. Once you have contacted one or both, you may want to seek a mental health or substance misuse professional. They can help you learn about the addiction process, including what triggers you to want to smoke and how relapse-prevention skills work. They may want to use hypnosis to help with thought patterns and negative behaviors. Cognitive behavioral therapy is also often used to teach a person to think more positively and to be aware of inner voices that may try to convince a person to relapse. Many professionals also use breathing exercises and grounding exercises to help a person with anxiety and depression symptoms. I definitely recommend that you ask your friends and family for support. I do not think we give enough credit to people who are trying to stop smoking. It is not an easy task, but it is done every day. I have no doubt that you will succeed. I wish you the best.

The doors we open and close each day decide the lives we live.
—Flora Whittemore

QUESTION:

Dear Andy,
Can you tell me how long it takes the average person to get clean from substances?
Sincerely,
Looking for Answers

ANSWER:

Dear Looking for Answers,
This is a very open question and is difficult to answer. First of all, what is your definition of clean? Some substances can take days to leave the body, while others can take weeks or even months. There are so many variables. It can depend on the type of substance a person uses, how much of the substance the person uses, and how long the person used the substance. If you are trying to get clean, it is important to have the support you need to stop using. I would suggest seeking a substance misuse professional for guidance in helping you through the process. No matter what the length of time, it will go by whether you are clean or not, so why not just go for it. I promise you will look back and be grateful that you cared enough about yourself to have a happy, ful-filled, and sober life. Take care, my friend.

The hero is the one who kindles a great light in the world, who sets up blazing torches in the dark streets of life for men to see by. The saint is the man who walks through the dark paths of the world, himself a light.
—Felix Adler

QUESTION:

Dear Andy,
My son has been acting different lately, and I am afraid that he may have an addiction problem. How do you determine whether a person has a problem with substances?
Sincerely,
Out of Sorts

ANSWER:

Dear Out of Sorts,
First and foremost, have you asked him? Many parents are afraid to bring this up, but communication can play a big part in helping your child stay free of drugs and alcohol. Have you looked in his room? Sometimes privacy can go out the window when you are concerned about your child's safety. There are many signs that may indicate the use of a mind-altering substance. Be mindful of signs of lethargy or enhanced energy, or changes in personality, such as becoming less talkative or more talkative. Watch for changes in behavior, such as hanging around with new friends, remaining isolated from others, or losing interest in his appearance and beginning to look unkempt. Make note if his grades go down in school. You might want to check his pupils to see if they are dilated or very tiny or if his eyes look red and/or glossy. You may notice that he tends to have itchy skin or that he is picking at his face. The list could go on and on, depending on the person and drug of choice. The best step you can take is to seek a substance misuse professional and learn about mind-altering substances. Such education may help you to determine if your son is using, and what skills you may need to help him if he does have an addiction. He may benefit from going to his medical doctor. You can ask his doctor for a urinalysis that can test for mind-altering substances. If your son absolutely refuses to take the test, there is a good chance he may be using a mind-altering substance. Good for you for being involved in your son's life. It is sad that many parents are in denial and would rather turn the other cheek. They may be thinking magical thoughts and hoping that the problem will go away on its own. Wishing you the best.

We must have the daring to be nothing but ourselves if we are to know what true power is.
—Danielle LaPorte

QUESTION:

Hello, Andy,
In watching the media, reading the papers, and listening to people talk, it seems to me that people who make less money are more apt to have problems with drugs. I guess I will ask. Is addiction more prevalent in lower-income populations?
Best,
Not Sure

ANSWER:

Dear Not Sure,
This is absolutely not the case. Thank you so much for asking this question, as there is a common misconception that substance abuse relates directly to income. However, addiction does not discriminate. Anyone can become addicted to mind-altering substances. I have seen people from all financial classes with substance addiction. I will add that people who have a lot of money have more access to substances because they have the financial means to purchase them. A lot of times people who have more financial means may purchase more expensive drugs, such as cocaine, oxycodone, and expensive liquors. People with less money may purchase less expensive drugs, such as crack cocaine, methamphetamines, heroin, and cheaper liquor. Financial class has nothing to do with this disease. I have seen people who were making high incomes lose their jobs and homes as their addictions progressed. It breaks my heart to see the devastating effects this disease has on so many people.

A heart can be broken, but it will keep beating just the same.
—Fanny Flagg

QUESTION:

Hello, Andy,
I have young children, and my biggest fear is that they may get involved with drugs when they are older. Is there a common gateway drug?
Sincerely,
Gateway

ANSWER:

Dear Gateway,

The most common gateway drug is cigarettes, and alcohol and marijuana often follow. I would suggest that you talk to your children about the dangers of drugs. I also suggest that you aim to serve as the best role model possible, and do not use cigarettes or any kind of mind-altering substances in front of your children. Model the person you hope they will become. Keep the lines of communication open so that they feel comfortable to discuss drugs with you, especially as they grow older. I can almost guarantee you that with time, your children will be exposed to drugs in some way. Peer pressure is nasty and devastating for our youth. By keeping the lines of communication open, your children may be more likely to discuss what they encounter and let you act as a supporter and educator of the dangers and implications of drugs. I hope this helps.

Accept yourself for who you are, both inside and out. As you let go of your false identity, you will be loved for who you really are, and, finally, those who gravitate toward you will appreciate the real you.
—Hayley Hobson

QUESTION:

Hello, Andy,
My eighteen-year-old son came home drunk last night and had been driving my car. I am not sure what to do. Do you think I should say something to him?
Sincerely,
Tongue Tied

ANSWER:

Dear Tongue Tied,
Yes, absolutely! I think you should tell him that you know he was under the influence of alcohol while driving your car. We are only as sick as our secrets. You need to be open with these things. Please explain to him that drinking and driving your car is a huge liability for both of you. He is fortunate that he did not hurt himself or someone else. Do you plan on taking his keys away? What will his consequence be from this action? This is not something that should be taken lightly! Many teens feel they are infallible because the part of the human brain that thinks through consequences is not completely developed at this age. Therefore, teens tend to take risks. Please discuss the penalties of drinking alcohol and driving. Please do not allow this to continue. Statistically, one of the highest death rates among teenagers in the United States is from driving automobiles while under the influence of mind-altering substances. Please help keep your child from becoming a statistic. The best of luck to you and your family.

If I could reach back through time and whisper something to that girl, it would simply be this: Be patient. Be kind to yourself. And wake up.
—Dani Shapiro

QUESTION:

Dear Andy,
I have noticed that since I stopped drinking six months ago, I am depressed and have very low energy. I have found myself withdrawing from friends and family. What can I do to make my life better?
Regards,
I'm Sick of This.

ANSWER:

Hello, I'm Sick of This,
I would recommend that you contact your medical doctor and find out if there is something he can do to help you. He may suggest antidepressants for a little while to help you get through some of these symptoms. When we are in early recovery, our brain goes through something called postacute withdrawal syndrome. This is when the brain begins to repair itself. In return, we may become moody, lethargic, anxious, and depressed. Exercise and a good, nutritious diet can help your brain and body to heal. I would also recommend that you attend substance misuse or mental health counseling to learn new skills to help you in early recovery. You may also benefit from group counseling. Statistics have shown that people in early recovery benefit from group counseling because they are able to talk to others who are experiencing the same symptoms. There is definitely something to be said for being with people who make you feel understood and accepted. Good for you for taking care of yourself. I promise things will get better with time.

It's all about hope, kindness, and a connection with one another.
—Elizabeth Taylor

QUESTION:

Dear Andy,

Recently I lost my son from a heroin overdose. I am so sad. I wish I could have done something different and often think this is my fault. All I think about is his death. I am isolating myself and feel pure sadness. Please give me some words that can make me get to a better place.

Lost Mom

ANSWER:

Dear Lost Mom,

I know that there are no words I could give you that could ever get rid of the pain you are feeling. This is not the first time a parent has asked me this question. The sad thing is that there is an epidemic of our young people overdosing on heroin. In New Hampshire, where I live, we lost more than three hundred people from heroin overdose in 2014. I am so scared to see what this next year will bring. Most parents tend to blame themselves. I have never met a parent who did not ask the question, "What could I have done differently?" Another one is "What did I do wrong?" The way you feel is shared among so many. I would recommend getting into mental health counseling, consulting your medical doctor to see if he or she can help you, and trying to find a grief support group of other parents who have gone through the same experience. A group of people who are going through a similar situation can be very helpful. There is nothing better than talking to someone who is in the same boat. I hope this helps. I wish I could take your pain away. God bless you and your family.

QUESTION:

Andy,
Someone told me that I am an ACOA because I am controlling. What does that mean?
ACO, I Guess

ANSWER:

Dear ACOA I Guess,
I believe they may be referring to an Adult Child of an Alcoholic (ACOA). Some people (not all) who were raised by an active alcoholic can have control issues when they become adults because when they were growing up, they may have felt that they had no control over their environment. So when they are older, they try to control their own personal environment. This may spill into personal relationships, employment, and day-to-day life. Some of these traits can be beneficial because a controlling person can be very organized and may be seen as a leader, but some of the traits can be harmful to the ACOA and that person's loved ones. This could cause friction and make it difficult for others to be around the ACOA. All relationships need to be balanced in order to be successful. If you do feel that you have control problems, I suggest that you get into counseling. Counseling can help you explore your controlling tendencies and help you to feel safe and comfortable in order to trust your environment. I wish you well.

It is easier to act yourself into a new way of feeling rather than feel your way into a new way of acting.
—G. D. Morgan

IT TAKES A WHOLE FAMILY TO HAVE A SUCCESSFUL RECOVERY

Over the years, I have worked with many family members who were devastated over their loved ones' addictions. From what parents have told me, every parent's worst nightmare is finding his or her child dead from an overdose of heroin. More than one has said to me, "I am afraid to kick him out because I am afraid of him dying in the street, and then I find myself afraid to keep him in the house because I am afraid to find him dead in his bedroom." I have heard from lots of husbands or wives that they have had enough of their spouses' drinking. Often a husband or wife will complain of the personality change undergone and the destruction caused when the spouse is under the influence. I have heard so many stories from so many different people and have found that most of those stories have strong commonalities. I have no doubt that addiction is a family disease. Once a family member is addicted to a mind-altering substance, the rest of the family can be affected with worry, despair, sadness, anxiety, and loneliness. If you or a loved one has a substance misuse issue, please do not hesitate to reach out to a professional for help.

I wish you the best, and thank you for reading my book.

ABOUT THE AUTHOR

Lori Magoon is a licensed clinical mental health clinician (LCMHC), master's-level licensed alcohol and drug counselor (MLADC), trained hypnotherapist, past talk show host of *Self-empowerment-NH*, and president and CEO of Self-empowerment-NH, LLC. Lori prides herself on empowering others to reach their fullest potential. Lori specializes in addiction in families by offering support and education to family members affected by alcoholism and drug addiction. Lori uses research-based practices to facilitate stronger family units and healthier relationships. Lori has dedicated her career to helping people change their negative perceptions to positive ones by opening the door to self-empowerment.

Just Ask Andy

Just Ask Andy is a collection of inquiries from people who have been affected by substance abuse and addiction, either directly or indirectly. Inspired by the Facebook popularity of "Andy," the quirky tabby cat rumored to have been addicted to catnip, this book integrates humor into a serious subject matter. Written by Lori Magoon, a veteran master's-level alcohol and drug counselor and radio show host, *Just Ask Andy* is a compilation of the most commonly asked questions by individuals who struggle with substance abuse and addiction and family members who are affected by an individual's substance abuse and addiction issues. Each question is accompanied by informative answers, real-world stories, and inspirational quotes. Prepare to laugh, cry, and become more knowledgeable about the roller-coaster ride to addiction recovery.